# Be a Friend

# Be a Friend

קנה לך חבר

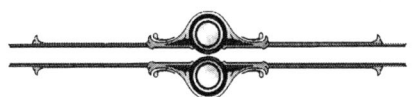

TARGUM/FELDHEIM

First published 2002
Copyright © 2002 by Moshe Goldberger
ISBN 1-56871-204-9
All rights reserved

No part of this publication may be translated, reproduced, stored in a retrieval system, or transmitted in any form or by any means, electronic, mechanical, photocopying, recording, or otherwise, without prior permission in writing from both the copyright holder and the publisher.

*Published by:*
TARGUM PRESS, INC.
22700 W. Eleven Mile Rd.
Southfield, MI 48034
E-mail: targum@netvision.net.il
Fax: 888-298-9992
www.targum.com

*Distributed by:*
FELDHEIM PUBLISHERS
202 Airport Executive Park
Nanuet, NY 10954
www.feldheim.com

*Printed in Israel*

This publication has been dedicated

by

# Hershey and Raisy Friedman

of Montreal, Canada

# Contents

*A Letter to a Friend* . . . . . . . . . . . . . 9
*Preface* . . . . . . . . . . . . . . . . . . . 11

## PART 1: Developing Friendships . . . . 17

1. Defining a Friend . . . . . . . . . 19
2. Teachers and Friends . . . . . . . 22
3. Spiritual Energy . . . . . . . . . . 25
4. Rebuking with Love . . . . . . . . 29
5. Praising Others . . . . . . . . . . 34
6. Turning the Tables . . . . . . . . 39
7. Giving and Receiving . . . . . . . 43
8. Smile . . . . . . . . . . . . . . . 47
9. Using Names . . . . . . . . . . . 51
10. Listening . . . . . . . . . . . . . 53
11. Acquiring Friends . . . . . . . . . 56
12. Avoiding Arguments . . . . . . . 60
13. The Wise Response . . . . . . . . 64
14. It Is Good to Admit . . . . . . . . 66
15. Kindly Greetings . . . . . . . . . 69
16. In Your Friend's Shoes . . . . . . 72

17. Motivating Others . . . . . . . . . . . . . 74
18. Be Yourself. . . . . . . . . . . . . . . . . 77
19. New Acquaintances . . . . . . . . . . . 79
20. "Peace Offering" . . . . . . . . . . . . . 82
21. Heads or Tails . . . . . . . . . . . . . . 84
22. Answering Questions. . . . . . . . . . 86
23. Picking Up Clues. . . . . . . . . . . . . 89
24. Word Power . . . . . . . . . . . . . . . 93
25. Getting Help . . . . . . . . . . . . . . . 97
26. Praising Properly . . . . . . . . . . . 100
27. On the Phone. . . . . . . . . . . . . . 103
28. Timing and Courtesy . . . . . . . . . 106
29. Six Questions. . . . . . . . . . . . . . 109
30. Choosing Friends . . . . . . . . . . . 111
31. Forgiveness . . . . . . . . . . . . . . 114

# PART 2: Ten Steps to *Shidduchim* . . 117

*Introduction* . . . . . . . . . . . . . . . . . . 119
1. Begin with Thanks . . . . . . . . . . . 121
2. Seeing the Future . . . . . . . . . . . 124
3. Growing Younger. . . . . . . . . . . . 127
4. Be Positive . . . . . . . . . . . . . . . 129
5. Self-Discipline . . . . . . . . . . . . . 132
6. Rejoice . . . . . . . . . . . . . . . . . 134
7. Relating to Others . . . . . . . . . . 136
8. Be Organized. . . . . . . . . . . . . . 139
9. Five Keys to Improvement. . . . . . 141
10. The Bottom Line . . . . . . . . . . . 146

# A Letter to a Friend

*In appreciation for inspiring the writing of this book*

Dear —,

"Acquiring a friend" (*Avos* 1:16) is a lifelong career and a deeply rich and rewarding experience. A close relationship of sharing, compromise, managing conflict, being flexible, taking responsibilities, and doing kindness develops a person and helps perfect him for this world and the next.

Communication, openness, and sharing enthusiasm for Torah and mitzvos are a joy for true friends who are sincere in their caring and sharing. A true friend is someone who is there for you no matter what, based on the mitzvah premise of loving others as oneself. Your friends will not leave you; the joy of the relationship will not end, just as one does not let go of himself.

The Gemara teaches, "Either a friend or death" (*Bava Basra* 16b). We learn that friendship is an essential component of life itself. With the assistance of good friends who are there for us every step of the way, we can develop ourselves and become great.

The research for this work and the challenge of writing it has helped me understand Hillel's teaching that the entire Torah stands on the principle of "Do not do to others something that is hateful to you." Hashem, our "very best Friend," has many messengers, agents who are sent to become our good friends and who make all the difference in our lives.

As a support system, a mentor, a sounding board, and a passionate fan, your insights, practicality, and encouragement were greatly appreciated, every step of the way.

Thank you for being a good friend and for representing many of the lessons that we have cited in this work.

May Hashem repay you for your friendship to me. May we all learn to love and respect each other, as the Torah teaches, and may we merit the complete redemption with *achdus*, speedily in our time.

Sincerely,

M. G.

# Preface

How important is it to you to learn how to get along with other people? Is dealing with people one of the biggest challenges in your daily life? Do you get along well with your parents, siblings, spouse, children, neighbors, shul-mates, friends, acquaintances, and strangers? How can you increase your level of enthusiasm in life for yourself, as well as in your dealings with others?

The world stands on three pillars, Torah, *avodah* (prayer), and kindness (*Avos* 1:2). Since each one represents one-third of the universe, we have to ask ourselves, do we invest sufficient effort in developing our skills for dealing kindly with others? There are definite mitzvah skills that we need to learn and practice in dealing with others. Some techniques are subtle and sensitive, but we can learn from the examples of our Sages how to interact with others in a smoother and more meaningful manner. There are ways to solidify our friendships with others and acquire qualities to perfect ourselves in these endeavors.

There are six questions that we will be asked by the Heavenly Court to be deemed worthy of entering the World to Come (*Shabbos* 31a). Three of these questions focus on how we interacted with others (see *Maharsha*).

➤ Have you dealt with others honestly?

➤ Did you get along well with your spouse and children?

➤ Were you involved in helping other people?

We are extremely fortunate that we possess the test questions in advance, since this enables us to be prepared with the right answers.

The Torah is rich with teachings of how Hashem wants us to deal with others. We need to analyze this information and relate to it in a practical way. Our sages in every generation have taught us great lessons in how to improve our dealings with each other. Their rules and guidelines will help us succeed in our daily lives.

How can you get the most out of these lessons? There are seven steps to take:

1. Apply the *mishnah*, "Drink their words with thirst" (*Avos* 1:4). Develop in yourself a driving desire, a vigorous determination to improve your skills in getting along with other people. How is this done? Keep reminding yourself of the great mitzvah, "Love your friend as yourself" (*Vayikra* 19:18). "This is the most fundamental mitzvah of the Torah" (*Shabbos* 31a).

2. Review each principle in this book at least ten times. Look up the sources in Tanach and Talmud and memorize the original words of our Sages.

3. Ask yourself when and how you can apply each lesson. Picture yourself applying what you have learned. Our Sages have taught us that a wise person always looks ahead to the future *(Tamid* 32a) in order to be prepared to act properly.

4. Prepare notes for yourself. Take them with you when you go out and review them as often as you can. We know a person who wrote down three principles he had learned on the topic of getting along with others and taped them to his car's steering wheel to review at red lights and when stuck in traffic. As the years passed, he accumulated many personal success stories that resulted from applying these lessons.

5. Share the lessons you learn with your family, friends, shul-mates, and coworkers. You will gain from this in that others will reciprocate and share lessons they have learned and experiences they have had with you. You will also inspire others to continue on their personal paths to perfection, helping them overcome obstacles they might be facing.

6. Use some of these lessons as a slogan of the week or the month for yourself and others. Our Sages used to say things repeatedly — "He used to say" (*Avos* 1:2, 3, 13, 14, and many more) — in order to live by them

always. Review your slogans daily and apply regularly, when you are confronted with an unsatisfied customer, a disgruntled spouse, or an angry friend.

7. Work with a *chavrusa* (study partner). Rabbeinu Yonah explains (in his commentary to *Avos* 1:6) that we need a partner for three areas: Torah study, assistance in mitzvah performance, and good advice. Joining forces with a friend will prove invaluable as you set out to improve your friendship skills.

With these seven steps, you can achieve greatness in being a friend. The chapters that follow will help you succeed in this most worthwhile endeavor.

# Part 1

# Developing Friendships

Chapter 1

# Defining a Friend

How do you go about acquiring a friend? The word *chaver*, friend, has the same root as the word *chibur*, connection. The Gemara mentions that "birds of a feather flock together" (*Chullin* 65a). When we want to know whether a newly discovered type of bird may be kosher or not, we have a clue by which birds it keeps company with. Similarly, people who feel comfortable in each other's presence tend to become friends.

If people sense you have the same values and the same interests as they do, they will like you more. This applies primarily to essential beliefs, but also to externals to a certain degree. People feel more comfortable if you have the same customs they do.

If we want to be accepted by certain people, we need to show that we are similar to them — whether it is by ascribing to certain beliefs or by dressing in a certain style. This makes people more comfortable and causes them to open up and relax. Of course, such behavior should only be adopted if it is in line with Torah values. When we see how similar we are to each and every loyal Jew, we will feel more comfortable around them and befriend them.

> *A person should not be awake among those who are sleeping, nor should he be asleep among those who are awake. He should not cry among those who are laughing, nor laugh among those who are crying. He should not stand among those who are sitting, nor sit among those who are standing.... The rule is, a person not be different from other people.*
>
> (*Derech Eretz Zuta*, ch. 5)

Be the same as others. Mingle with them so that they will feel comfortable around you. To become friends with someone, you need to adopt his way of doing things to a certain degree.

# Defining a Friend

Friends are tuned into each other's wavelength. If you want someone to be your friend, recognize his values and belief system and respect them. We learn in *Mishlei*, "Walking with the sages will make you wise" (*Mishlei* 13:20). Similarly, walking with someone (in a figurative sense) will develop a friendship. Walking together develops a rapport, a meeting of the minds.

Chapter 2

# Teachers and Friends

The step before "acquire for yourself a friend" is "accept upon yourself a teacher" (*Avos* 1:6). We need both teachers and associates in life. Such relationships are worth their weight in gold. When you have a teacher, rebbe, or coach, you will always have assistance in getting where you want to go.

In every area of life it is beneficial to have the guidance of others — in your family setting, yeshivah, community, and workplace. Co-workers and associates can help you meet your deadlines and deliver quality products and services. You can help them in turn with advice and tips that will make their lives easier and more productive.

Discussing plans with a good friend, a

friend who can motivate you and share his ideas with you, works wonders. A friend can guide you and objectively evaluate your spiritual growth and success. Together, you can use your combined brainpower to help each other solve problems that alone you would not be able to work out.

Other people can be there for you. Learn to admit to your ignorance and ask others for help. People want to learn new skills and new insights. They want to know how they're doing and how they can improve.

Your spouse can be your best friend. As the person who cares the most about you, he or she serves as your constant support. If you are human, as we all are, you don't know everything. But it is difficult to admit it. You need other people's input on a regular basis. It takes training to get along with others and accept their help, but that is what the Mishnah instructs us to do. "Who is wise? He who learns from every person" (*Avos* 4:1).

*I have learned much from my teachers, more*

*from my colleagues, and the most from my disciples.*

(*Taanis* 7b)

The more we learn from others, the more we grow.

## Chapter 3

# Spiritual Energy

*Two are better than one.*

(*Koheles* 4:9)

Why would Shlomo HaMelech, the wisest man of all time, teach us something that seems so obvious? Commentaries explain that the verse is not merely teaching that two people, with their combined strength, can accomplish more as a team. Rather, there is a synergetic force which enables both of them to accomplish much more than each by himself.

We will benefit greatly from analyzing the process of growing through joining with others and working as a team to conquer and overcome challenges.

The core of our body is the *neshamah*, the

spiritual entity that keeps us alive. We can control our bodies with our thoughts, which have their source in the *neshamah*. When you interact with others, it is not merely a physical connection; your *neshamah* is also connecting with their *neshamos*.

Hashem created you and charged you with a purposeful mission. He provides challenges in the form of weaknesses and limitations, and He provides you with ways to overcome these challenges, to change and move forward.

Part of the arsenal that Hashem has prepared for you are the people surrounding you, the friends and family members who support you and coach you to success. Through talking with others, counseling, support, and pep talks, you will be able to leave behind that which is self-destructive and inhibiting your growth. Others can help you reinforce your own willpower, overcome your old habits, and become a new person.

Align yourself with others to produce spiritual energy that will elevate you. As you acquire

# Spiritual Energy

a friend, you yourself become more powerful.

The Talmud (*Berachos* 10a) gives us five comparisons between Hashem and our souls:

1. Hashem fills the world; our soul fills the body.
2. Hashem is invisible, as is the soul.
3. Hashem sustains the world; the soul sustains the body.
4. Hashem is pure; so is the soul.
5. Hashem resides in a hidden chamber; so does the soul.

Our soul has unlimited power and potential. It is actually a portion of the *Shechinah*. We need to plug into and access this power, the invisible, eternal part of our being.

Our soul's purpose is to emulate and praise Hashem, sustain and energize the body, and enable the body to serve Hashem properly.

The mitzvah to love others as we love ourselves becomes clearer when we understand this concept. We all have a *neshamah* that connects us spiritually to Hashem and to each other. The way we treat others is essentially the way we are treating a portion of ourselves!

The spiritual essence of a person is not interested in physical acquisitions. Instead, the purpose of life is to acquire spiritual acquisitions. When we make friendships, our goal should be to connect with others in a way that will empower each person to develop his full potential in the service of Hashem. N this way, we will be furthering our goals in this world in the best way possible.

Chapter 4

# Rebuking with Love

One of the greatest mitzvos of the Torah is "Love your friend as yourself" (*Vayikra* 19:18). It is the source of Hillel's famous teaching, "Treat others as you would like to be treated."

Not only does the Torah instruct us to love each other, but in addition, the verse immediately before it commands, "Do not hate your brother in your heart" (*Vayikra* 19:17).

But who would hate his brother or sister? The verse continues: "Give rebuke to your friend, but do not bear sin because of him."

When we criticize or correct someone we can be performing a mitzvah, but only if it is done appropriately, as an expression of love, not hate. If you hurt a person's feelings, lowering his self-esteem, you will arouse resentment and anger. We learn from the Torah that hurting a person's self-esteem is worse than taking his life (see *Avos* 3:15).

As with all mitzvos, we need to learn how to fulfill the mitzvah of rebuke correctly. Merely criticizing and condemning others without offering them Torah guidelines will not be effective in the long run. Rambam teaches that one is obligated to offer constructive criticism privately, in a pleasant tone of voice, as a way of helping the person (*Hilchos Dei'os* 6:7).

Most of the time when people sin they do so under the premise that they were acting properly, either through lack of knowledge or through rationalization. This makes the mitzvah to help others improve a very difficult one. The rewards are great, but the risks of hurting someone in the process are also great. Rashi says, "Be careful not to embarrass the person in public when you offer rebuke."

Moshe Rabbeinu, the greatest leader of the Jewish people, had reason to deliver rebuke three times in his years of leadership: when two people left over some of their portion of manna (*Shemos* 16:20), when the *kohanim* did not eat of the offerings (*Vayikra* 10:16), and when the warriors returned from the war against Midyan without killing all the sinful women (*Bemidbar* 31:14). Yet in these three places, when Moshe reacted with a display of anger, he came to error (*Sifri, Bemidbar* 157).

We should avoid criticizing others as much as possible. It is necessary to be angry at transgressions of the Torah, but it is also necessary to beware of errors that can result even from justified anger. Hashem wants our anger to be directed at the action, not at the person who transgressed, even when the person shows a defiant attitude to what was right and insists on doing wrong. When we offer rebuke it is not to be delivered out of anger, but out of a desire to help the person.

When we see someone who needs to correct himself, before immediately reacting, we should think, *Why not begin with myself first? It will be more profitable and less dangerous.* The Gemara teaches us, "A person should adorn himself and then adorn others" (*Bava Basra* 60b).

The Talmud relates (*Bava Basra* 60a) that a Sage was asked if a certain practice was permitted. The Sage declined to respond and asked the questioner to return the following day, when he would answer him. The next day, upon the questioner's return, the Sage said that the practice was prohibited. It was soon revealed that the Sage had the prohibited situation in his own home but had taken steps to rectify it before he issued his ruling.

When you do need to correct someone, take steps to ensure that you are doing it properly. Begin by saying quietly to yourself as if you are speaking to the person that you would like to correct, "I love you! You are my brother!"

The Talmud explains that one of the reasons Jerusalem was destroyed was a lack of sufficient rebuke between people (*Shabbos* 119b). This lack was considered such a severe sin because it demonstrated a lack of caring and love

# Rebuking with Love

for each other. When we love someone, we strive to help him improve.

It is important to note that some people do not take kindly to rebuke them, and thus criticizing them may not be possible or advisable. We must learn to be diplomatic in handling people. Fools criticize, condemn, and complain. Wise people develop their own character to be understanding and forgiving. "Who is mighty? He who conquers his inclination" (*Avos* 4:1).

Never get into the habit of finding faults with others. Learn patience and understanding instead. Figure out why people do what they do. When we are about to criticize or rebuke someone, we should remember the beginning of the verse in *Vayikra* 19:17: "Do not hate your brother in your heart."

Chapter 5

# Praising Others

Mesilas Yesharim explains that pleasure is the ultimate objective of our stay in this world. The only way to achieve the ultimate pleasure is through performing mitzvos.

One of the greatest mitzvos is *chesed* — to help others. To be sensitive to their needs and to provide them with health, safety, food, a home, a *shidduch*, and, most of all, a feeling of importance. One of a person's deepest needs is to feel important, to feel that someone cares about him. When you praise someone, even with a small compliment, you are performing a great mitzvah of kindness.

When Avraham Avinu dealt with people, he would honor them greatly, calling them "my master" and referring to himself as "your servant" (*Bereishis* 18:3). It may seem that he was lowering his own dignity, but in reality he was raising himself to the greatest heights a person can reach in this world. Avraham's desire and his actions to help others in need made him a royal prince in the eyes of the Creator. We learn from Avraham how much effort we must invest in practicing kindness and humility to all.

Imagine how our lives would be transformed if we emulated Avraham's acts of kindness to others. When the Rambam defines the mitzvah to love every Jew as oneself, he begins, "We must relate their praise!" (*Hilchos Dei'os* 6:3).

Are we lavish in our praise of others? Why not? People do better work, with greater effort, when we approve of them.

Imagine how your home life would improve if you called your spouse at your lunch break, or right now, to say, "I've been thinking about your special qualities. You are so good to me...."

Everyone needs appreciation and encouragement for his self-esteem. Our Sages (*Bava Basra* 9b) teach that one who provides a poor person with money is performing a great mitzvah, which Hashem rewards with six superlative blessings. One who adds kind words of appreciation and encouragement is rewarded with eleven blessings. (*Tosafos* says that these eleven are in addition to the six already received, for a total of seventeen! Hence, one receives nearly twice as many blessings for adding kind words as he does for giving the money!)

Just as money given has to be authentic, so that the poor person can buy food and other needs, the praise and encouragement have to be sincere, from the heart.

The Prophet Yeshayah depicts the merits of saying kind words in the following way: "If you bring forth your soul to the needy, your light will shine…. Hashem will lead you always and satisfy your soul…" (*Yeshayah* 58:10). We see that true praise has to come from within our soul. We need to stop thinking about ourselves for a while and focus on another person's qualities.

Sincere praise is a form of wealth. It can transform your children, your spouse, and all those who surround you.

It is said that there are two kinds of people, those who say, "It's good to see you," and those who say, "I'm here." We need to train ourselves to become like the first type, focused more on other people and their needs.

Notice other people's virtues. Imagine if you could feed starving people — wouldn't you do so? Now realize that there are people all around you who are starved for your recognition. Wake up to their needs and recognize the opportunities you have to perform kindness.

How many gas stations do you pass as you drive to and from work? Consider this exercise: each station can remind you that fuel is necessary in order to keep going. People also need to be noticed and appreciated in order to survive and thrive. That is their fuel.

One of the keys to humility is to recognize that every person we meet is superior to us in some way. This should inspire us to analyze the good in others and learn from them, as the Mishnah says, "Who is wise? He who learns from every person" (*Avos* 4:1). Then strive to acknowledge these qualities by offering compliments and praises to others.

## Chapter 6

# Turning the Tables

*You [Hashem] open Your hand and satiate the desires of all the living.*

(*Tehillim* 145:16)

We are obligated to emulate the Creator. Thus, we need to help others by providing them with their needs and desires, just as Hashem provides us with our needs and desires.

When you want someone to do something for you, you are most likely to succeed if you speak to him about his own needs and how they can best be filled by doing the thing you desire him to do. For example, in order to convince someone to stop smoking, you could launch into a tirade about how smoke nauseates you and how smokers are so grossly inconsiderate, or you can discuss in a calm, rational way some of the smoker's goals in life. Will smoking help him achieve any of his lifelong dreams and aspirations? Won't it, in fact, hurt him? If you can get the smoker to understand this and arouse in him a strong desire to stop smoking for his own benefit, you will succeed!

Beis Shammai and Beis Hillel, two of the greatest yeshivos in our history, had many debates in their time. After one three-year debate on an issue of halachah, they merited to hear a *bas kol* (heavenly voice) proclaim: "These and those are the words of the living God, but the halachah follows Beis Hillel." The Gemara explains that this is because they were more flexible and patient, and they would study and review the words of their opponents first (*Eiruvin* 13b).

Many times, we try to persuade others to our way of thinking. Do we consider how to get them to want to listen to us? This *gemara* provides us with the secret to achieving success. Learn to understand the other person's point of view, to see his angle, before you push for your own.

People are most interested in solving their own problems and challenges. When you show them how you can help them cope, they will be receptive to listening to you. In business or at work, they will be eager to buy your merchandise or service. At home, your family members will be appreciative and attentive.

The Gemara teaches that the verse "You open Your hand and satiate the desires of all the living" is the most significant verse in *Ashrei* (*Berachos* 4b). This is one of the reasons that one who says *Ashrei* three times a day is guaranteed a portion in the World to Come. This teaches us how important it is to help others get what they need and want. Figure out what others need and you will have a great key to emulating Hashem.

When people see that you care about them and their needs, they feel good about themselves and will respond positively. You can also let them feel that they reached the decision to improve on their own. This will make them feel even better and will not harm you at all.

"All those who humble themselves will be elevated by Hashem" (*Eiruvin* 13b). When you suggest an idea and allow others to take the credit, Hashem will help you succeed greatly.

Chapter 7

# Giving and Receiving

*Who is wise? He who learns from every person. Who is honored? He who honors others.*

(Avos 4:1)

One of the secrets to gaining friends is to realize how much you can learn from every individual in the world. If you are interested in others, they will automatically warm up to you and become interested in you.

This may sound a little deceptive, but in actuality Hashem gave us the mitzvah to love each other "as we love ourselves" to teach us a core principle for success in this area. When you like others, they will like you and help you. They will sense your feelings and respond.

We have to constantly remind ourselves to be grateful to all the people we interact with for the help they provide. Our customers and clients help us make a living. If we give them the best service, they will return for more, pay willingly for quality service and products, and enjoy what we offer.

Imagine telling yourself on the way to shul, "I love my shul-mates and all other Jews." Not only will this greatly enhance the quality of your prayers, but it will also improve your interactions with those around you.

On the way home from shul, you can say, "I love my wife and family." They are created in Hashem's image, and they do so much for you. When you are conscious of this, you will treat your family members with more love and respect, and this love and respect will be reciprocated to you.

On the way to work, think about your love for your coworkers and your customers. In addition to fulfilling the mitzvah to love others, you will also be gaining specific benefits for yourself.

*Greet every person with a thoughtful, pleasant countenance.*

(Avos 1:15)

This *mishnah* is teaching us how to win friends. We need to greet all people with excitement and enthusiasm. Show that you are pleased to see them. Your tone of voice and your facial expression says a lot.

*As water reflects one's face, so a person's heart reflects another's.*

(Mishlei 27:19)

However, demonstrating love and honor for others should not be done merely for the practical benefits which result. The greater, overriding purpose in loving and honoring others is to serve Hashem.

The Talmud teaches, "One who greets his fellowman with 'shalom' before prayers in the morning is considered to be treating him as an altar for idol worship" (*Berachos* 14a). Before prayers one may say, "Good morning," but he should avoid saying "Shalom aleichem" (*Shulchan Aruch, Orach Chaim* 89:2).

This halachah teaches us an important lesson. After we pray and acknowledge that we live to serve Hashem, we have a mitzvah to greet all others. Because we are in Hashem's service, we honor and respect all humans, who were created in His image! (Rav Avigdor Miller, *Rejoice O Youth*, p. 375).

# Chapter 8

# Smile

We would not dream of going out in public without first dressing up. We don our clothes and hat, polish our shoes, and decorate further with tasteful accessories. But sometimes we forget to don the most important part of our attire: a pleasant facial expression.

> *Showing the white of your teeth to a fellowman is more beneficial than offering a glass of milk.*
> (*Kesubos* 111b)

Your smile speaks volumes. It declares, "I'm happy to see you" and helps you fulfill the *mishnah*, "Greet every person with joy" (*Avos* 3:16).

The essence of a heartwarming smile is your inner joy. If you are speaking over the phone, is it still important to smile? Yes. First of all, Hashem still sees how you are fulfilling the *mishnah*'s lesson. Second, you yourself feel happier when you smile at others. Third, your smile comes through the phone lines, through your voice and choice of expressions.

If someone would offer you five dollars for every smile, how many times a day would you manage to smile? In reality, Hashem offers much more than five dollars.

How can you smile when you are not in the mood to do so? Perhaps that is why our Sages don't just say, "Smile." They say, "Show the white of your teeth to your fellowman." This is a specific action that you can perform even without feelings. Force yourself to show others your teeth, and you will become happy.

When you smile and say, "Hi, how are you?" people brighten up and your own day can improve immensely. You can have a positive mental attitude and be of good cheer. Our teachers have said that a person's face is considered as a public domain. Make sure you don't harm others and ruin their day by leaving a scowl on your face.

A smile is a mitzvah that costs little and creates a lot. It enriches those who see it and those who give it; it takes but a moment, but lasts forever. We all need them, whether we are rich or poor, for the home, business, and in the street. It is a form of sunshine which nurtures, sustains, and heals, and it can be produced on demand with Hashem's help.

Are we saying that one should smile nonstop? Actually, no. The Mishnah instructs us: "Greet every person with a thoughtful, pleasant countenance" (*Avos* 1:15). It is better not to enter a room smiling because the person seeing you may think you always have a fixed smile plastered on your face. Let the person see you first thinking about him and then radiating a joyous smile of recognition.

As with other mitzvos, we must practice to perfect and fine-tune our smile so that it is sincere, warm, and authentic.

Another ingredient in this formula for kindness to others is to turn our face toward our fellowman. With positive eye contact we convey feelings of respect and affection to others. When someone approaches you, stop what you are doing, think about the person, turn your eyes and face to him, and smile.

When you treat others with respect and deference, they will reciprocate. When you offer people who meet you a warm smile and turn in their direction, they will think to themselves, *He likes me!* They will happily receive your message, "You are special to me" and respond in kind.

Chapter 9

# Using Names

We find throughout the Torah that when Hashem spoke to Moshe, Avraham, or any of the other prophets, He always called them first by name. We can do the same. When a person hears you address him by name, he is pleased and flattered. It is a subtle way of recognizing someone and showing interest in him — you cared enough to remember his name.

The fact that a person's name is important to him is sufficient reason to perform the kindness of using it. People are proud of their names. If you find it difficult to remember names, you can think of a hint for yourself, for example, a connection to Tanach, that will make it easier to remember. Perhaps a person's name is Avraham — find a certain trait that he has in common with Avraham Avinu.

It does take some focus, time, and energy to register a name and use it properly, but like all good things, the efforts are well worthwhile. Not only will you make people feel special, but you will also trigger memories of their parents and dear ones calling them by name.

The *rosh yeshivah* of one of the largest institutions in the world today is said to know the names of all of his thousands of disciples. They love him for it, and it surely makes a great difference in his interactions with them.

Rashi (on *Vayikra* 1:1) writes that calling someone by his name is, in itself, a term of endearment. The word for "name" in Hebrew is *sheim*, which is similar to *sham* (there). A name defines the essence of the person — who is there. The more we focus on others, the greater kindness it is to them.

# Chapter 10

# Listening

Another key to showing others that you appreciate them is listening. In order to listen well, one has to focus on the person speaking to him and pay attention. When you listen to others, you are performing the kindness of making them feel important.

Listening is not merely keeping quiet; it is devoting your ears, eyes, mind, and heart to another person. It also leads to wisdom, as *Pirkei Avos* teaches: "Silence is a fence for wisdom" (*Avos* 3:17). You will always gain more wisdom through listening than through talking. Hashem gave us two ears but only one mouth to remind us to engage in more listening than talking (Gra on *Mishlei* 11:2).

If you are a good listener, people will like you more and more.

Concentrating your attention on one person at a time is a tremendous gift to that person.

The Mishnah in *Avos* (5:9) describes a wise person in seven ways, most of which are related to being a good listener:

1. He does not speak in the presence of one who is greater than he (i.e., he listens).

2. He does not interrupt (again, because he listens).

3. He does not rush to reply (he waits for the message to sink in before responding).

4. He asks relevant questions and answers accurately (showing that he has listened attentively).

5. He answers the first thing first and the last thing last (realizing that what was said first is more important to the speaker).

6. He acknowledges his lack of knowledge (thus encouraging the speaker to explain fully).

7. He admits the truth (the speaker surely appreciates this honesty and feels the time spent talking to him is worthwhile.)

If you think about it, why should a person care how much you know, if he doesn't think you care about him?

To win friends, you need to learn how to listen to them. In the great Yeshivah of Kelm, people would not speak until after they had asked, "Have you finished making your point?"

## Chapter 11

# Acquiring Friends

*Accept upon yourself a teacher, acquire for yourself a friend, and judge every person favorably.*

(*Avos* 1:6)

We know that having a teacher and judging others favorably are two foundations for success. It is surprising to find "acquire for yourself a friend" included in this list. We learn that we cannot possibly live a Torah-true life without proper friends.

According to the Rambam on this *mishnah*, it is worth it to even pay someone to be your friend. Our Sages consider friends so essential that they have told us, "Give me a *chavrusa* (companion) or give me death" (*Taanis* 23a).

## Acquiring Friends

How does one "buy" friends? The key is to show interest in the other person and discuss topics that interest him.

We find that when people call or write to us about our books, they are usually most enthusiastic about topics that interest them.

Yehoshua, who was chosen to lead the Jewish nation after Moshe Rabbeinu's passing, was selected because he had the ability to show interest in others. Hashem instructs Moshe, "Take Yehoshua, a man with the spirit in him" (*Bemidbar* 27:18). Rashi explains that this means he was able to adjust and relate to the spirit of each person.

We have mentioned before how essential it is to greet every person with joy, interest, and a pleasant countenance. Another mishnah (*Avos* 4:20) teaches that we should always be first to greet every person.

There is an obvious theme in these teachings: always make other people feel important. Every person was created in Hashem's image. Every Jew is considered Hashem's child. Approval, recognition, praise, and compliments are so vital.

The Mishnah does not say: "Greet *everyone* with a pleasant, thoughtful countenance"; rather, it says, "Greet *every person*." We must think of every person as a very important individual. When you meet someone new, imagine a good friend or someone you really appreciate and then transfer those feelings to this individual you do not know yet.

Saying "please," "thank you," and "I'm sorry" are all components in showing how significant we consider others. In *Fortunate Nation*, Rav Avigdor Miller, *zt"l*, explains that the verse, "You are children of Hashem" (*Devarim* 14:1), is one of the most thunderous declarations in Hashem's Torah. Three principles can be learned from it:

1. Hashem does solely what is good for His children.
2. We should always seek to emulate Him, as a son emulates his father.
3. We must be well-groomed and well-behaved in honor of Hashem.

Keeping these principles in mind will make acquiring friends far easier. Discuss with people the topics that interest them and show that you value them. You will be thus fulfilling the *mishnah*'s directive, "acquire for yourself a friend."

Chapter 12

# Avoiding Arguments

*Do not be like Korach and his congregation.*
(*Bemidbar* 17:5)

*Anyone who promotes or maintains disharmony transgresses a Torah prohibition.*
(*Sanhedrin* 110a)

Sometimes we attempt to display our superiority by correcting others and trying to prove they are wrong. We need to stop and ask ourselves, What is the purpose? Why argue with people and cause them discomfort and embarrassment?

The Rambam writes (*Moreh Nevuchim* 3:33): "One should listen to other people's words and not be obstinate…as it says: 'Don't stiffen your neck' (*Devarim* 10:16)."

Knowing how to refrain from talking and

# Avoiding Arguments

how to avoid verbal dissension is a very valuable skill. The Sage Shimon ben Gamliel told us, "All my life I was raised amongst the Sages and I did not find anything better for the body than silence" (*Avos* 1:17). We are also taught to become disciples of Aharon, to always love and pursue peace (*Avos* 1:12).

If you argue with and contradict others, you may win the battle sometimes, but you will never win the war because the friction that develops may cause you to lose a friend. The more we argue with others, attempting to set them straight, the more they will try to assert themselves and their authority by fighting back. If, on the other hand, you admit the other person's importance and leave him be, he will calm down, too. "A gentle response will turn back anger" (*Mishlei* 15:1).

When you yourself are corrected, admit to the truth. Express your thanks for points brought to your attention that you did not think about. It is great to be saved from making a mistake.

When it comes to learning Torah, we do encourage discussions and disputes. When these arguments are *l'sheim Shamayim* (for the sake of Heaven), as by Beis Hillel and Beis Shammai (*Avos* 5:20), they are ideal.

Beis Hillel and Beis Shammai's goals were to uncover the truth in Hashem's Torah, with respect to each other's right to a different opinion. Korach, on the other hand, argued for the sake of his own honor. For attempting to destroy Moshe Rabbeinu, who was considered the foundation of the earth, he was punished by being swallowed by the earth. The punishment was extremely appropriate because Korach attacked Moshe verbally, with his mouth, and the earth swallowed him by opening its "mouth."

The Talmud points out that Beis Hillel and Beis Shammai were always friendly and affectionate toward each other and they did not refrain from marrying into each other (*Yevamos* 14b). We also learned that Beis Hillel was careful to listen to Beis Shammai's view first and then to study their teachings carefully before voicing their own opinions (*Eiruvin* 13b). Because of these actions, the Gemara says that Beis Hillel merited to have the final halachah follow their position in most cases.

When you love and pursue peace, you are always a winner.

Chapter 13

# The Wise Response

How many times do we tell someone off, only to discover subsequently that we were wrong and they were right? Our Sages teach us a simple trick that can spare us a lot of heartache and guarantee us that we will be right most of the time. Right at the beginning of Shas we are taught a lesson that can help us throughout our lifetime: "Train your tongue to say, 'I don't know,' lest you be caught saying something false" (*Berachos* 4a).

"Who is wise? He who learns from every person" (*Avos* 4:1). How can you learn if you think you know it all already? We must learn not to be embarrassed to say, "I don't know."

But what about honesty? Don't you have to tell the truth when you do know a lot about the subject under discussion? *Tosafos* (on *Kiddushin* 30a) explains that one should always pretend ignorance in worldly matters. However, when it comes to Torah matters, one should be ready to teach others.

When you tell others they are wrong, they will usually become resentful, defensive, and perhaps even determined to prove you wrong. Thus, you should do your best to avoid telling someone when you think he has erred unless it will affect him in the future.

If someone purchased a garment that is unbecoming on him or unknowingly overpaid for an item that he is unable to return, the halachah requires us to praise the item to the unfortunate buyer (*Kesubos* 17a). We are not permitted to tell him that his new purchase is ugly or overpriced. The Torah way is to be "ignorant" when necessary, in order to protect another person's feelings and maintain friendships.

Chapter 14

# It Is Good to Admit

Which verse is the "most startling of all the statements in the Torah"? Rabbi Avigdor Miller (*A Kingdom of Cohanim*, p. 116) says it is *Vayikra* 10:20, where Moshe Rabbeinu admitted his error in criticizing his brother, Aharon.

This incident was planned by Hashem to teach us that Moshe was not ashamed to admit his error. It reinforces the fact that everything else Moshe said was without any error. Moshe Rabbeinu, the most extraordinary person in all of history, was still human, and even the greatest are capable of error when they are not speaking in prophecy.

Moshe admitted his error quickly, openly, and wholeheartedly. "It was good in his eyes," the Torah declares (ibid.).

When you accept blame upon yourself, others are more likely to have compassion for you. It takes courage, character, and training to admit your error quickly and emphatically, but it is well worth it.

"Anyone who passes over his personal feelings to forgive others is forgiven for all his sins" (*Rosh HaShanah* 17a). What a tremendous vote of approval Hashem bestows on those who humbly submit to others and strive to always get along with them!

Another area in which we are taught to overcome our emotions for the sake of Heaven is the Torah's emphasis on helping even so-called "enemies": "If you find your enemy's ox that has strayed, return it to him. If you see your enemy's donkey buckling under its burden, do not restrain yourself from unloading it" (*Shemos* 23:4–5).

"If your friend needs help to unload [his animal] and your enemy needs help to load, help your enemy first in order to overcome your evil inclination" (*Bava Metzia* 32b).

When we have trouble getting along with certain people, we must realize that Hashem is testing us. We need to overcome our negative feelings and be especially friendly to the unfriendly. "According to the difficulty, so is the reward" (*Avos* 5:23).

Chapter 15

# Kindly Greetings

*Be first to greet every person.*

(*Avos* 4:20)

When Yaakov Avinu came to Charan, he saw a group of shepherds relaxing near the well. Before criticizing them for wasting time from work, he asked, "My brothers, where are you from?" (*Bereishis* 29:4). This beginning conveys feelings of friendship and interest. Yaakov was acknowledging the shepherds as people of significance.

We must learn from Yaakov to begin a conversation with expressions of positivity, gentleness, and friendship.

"The words of the wise, when spoken gently, are accepted" (*Koheles* 9:17). We would have thought that the key is speaking with wisdom, but no, *Koheles* emphasizes, it is speaking with gentleness that causes people to change their minds and accept your message.

Yaakov Avinu asked the shepherds three questions before he got to his criticism: 1) Where are you from? 2) Do you know Lavan? 3) Is he at peace? The shepherds answered each question in turn — "We are from Charan...we know him...he is at peace."

Why all this shmoozing? Why does the Torah find it necessary to record this seemingly inconsequential information?

We learn that when we begin to discuss some issue with others, we should begin at points of agreement rather than at the point of disagreement. It is important to start building a relationship with casual small talk. Put the other person at ease before you go on to less pleasant or more serious topics.

This technique is useful for all your dealings, with your spouse, children, customers, friends, relatives, neighbors, or even strangers. Always open your conversations with friendliness, instead of with a direct confrontation. Look at things from the other person's viewpoint and think how you can work with them.

Chapter 16

# In Your Friend's Shoes

*Do not judge your friend until you have reached his place.*

(Avos 2:5)

It is easier to notice other people's faults than our own. We tend to have a blind spot to our own mistakes, yet we know that we are not born fully developed. It takes a lot of experience and practice to become an expert at anything. We should be equally understanding of other people's flaws.

Sometimes we want to motivate people to improve themselves. Our automatic reflex may be to admonish or scold sharply, but we must realize that this is not a very successful method of bringing about change. Put yourself in the other person's shoes and imagine how you would want to be told about a flaw that you have.

Our Father in Heaven, the Creator of the universe, teaches us that in situations where we must criticize someone, it is essential to begin with praise. When Hashem criticized Shaul, He praised him first (*Shmuel II* 21:1; see *Yevamos* 78b).

It is always easier to listen to unpleasant words after hearing about our good points. This follows the concept we discussed above that the best method of communication is through love. Focus on loving the person and you will be able to view and discuss his faults in a positive vein.

If you compliment someone, you will get his attention. It is important, however, to mean what you say. If the listener suspects that the praise is insincere and merely a lead-in to criticism, your words will fall on deaf ears.

Put yourself in the other person's position and think how the criticism will sound to him. Stress your words of praise and then switch subtly to the need for minor improvement to be worthy of more praise. In this way, the criticism is low-key and indirect, and your friendship is intact.

Chapter 17

# Motivating Others

Each of us is born with unique gifts, with areas in which we can more readily excel. Our most important job is to develop these areas within ourselves and to also help others do the same.

How can we help others develop their potential? The key is encouragement. When Yehoshua took over the leadership of the Jewish nation, Hashem fortified him many times with the words "*chazak ve'ematz,*" be strong and fortified. We too can shower others with words of praise and encouragement, thereby inspiring them to keep on improving.

Do not just offer constructive criticism after you see someone has fallen. It is a far greater mitzvah to support, encourage, and motivate others so that they won't fall in the first place. A word of cheerful praise brightens up one's day and warms the spirit.

Think back to a time when a few words of praise gave you the boost you needed to continue in a difficult path or tackle a new challenge. You can do the same for others. Moshe Rabbeinu, the greatest leader of the Jewish people, wanted to turn down the opportunity offered him by Hashem to serve as Hashem's messenger, but Hashem encouraged him to step up to the position.

We all need praise and recognition to reinforce the good things we do and to help us deal with life's challenges. When we praise even small improvements we notice in others, we promote their growth. Be specific in your praise and you will help others more.

You have the ability to encourage your spouse, children, and others around you. When you point out a person's outstanding past performance or potential future accomplishments, you will jump-start that person's vision of himself. A positive self-image can make all the difference.

In the very beginning of history, Hashem declared: "Let *us* create man" (*Bereishis* 1:26). He used this wording to teach us a striking lesson in humility and courtesy: A leader should always consult his staff and ask their permission before rendering decisions (*Rashi, loc. cit.*). We need to emulate this approach in our dealings with others.

Most people resist taking orders. They prefer to have input in the decision-making process. Even if you have already decided what to do, it never hurts to ask, "What do you think about this idea?"

People need to feel important. When they have been included in the decision, they will cooperate more and with better results. Keep in mind, also, that as human beings we always need input from each other. "Who is wise? He who learns from every person" (*Avos* 4:1).

The greatest gift you can give others is to bring out the best in them. Treat them as if you already see it happening.

## Chapter 18

# Be Yourself

*Every person is obligated to say, "Because of me, Hashem created the world."*

(Sanhedrin 37a)

What a stunning declaration! Do we truly understand this message, accept who we are, and recognize that we have the power to reach our goals?

Are you happy with your life? Do you feel comfortable with who you are or do you find yourself trying to conform to others and forcing yourself into a pattern that is not for you? Study your own personality and develop your individuality.

We all have talents and skills that make us unique, but we need to develop them. No one can do it for you. As the Sage Hillel always said,

"If I am not for myself, who will be for me?" (*Avos* 1:14).

It is said that the biggest mistake people make when applying for a job is not being themselves. Be yourself. There is no one exactly like you. Each of your experiences in life are uniquely yours. Hashem placed you in a certain family and a particular environment to enable you to become the best you.

This concept can be applied as well to other people. Your spouse, children, friends, and co-workers are also unique people with unique personalities. Encourage every person to develop his maximum potential and not to imitate others.

Shlomo HaMelech teaches, "Educate the child according to his way" (*Mishlei* 22:6). With our children we have to be particularly careful to encourage individuality. Each child is his own person and must be taught this.

Be yourself — and don't impose your will on others. Allow them to be themselves, too.

## Chapter 19

# New Acquaintances

The Mishnah in *Avos* (2:13) lists five qualities that five Sages recommended to lead one to "the good pathway for life": a good eye, a good friend, a good neighbor, seeing ahead, and a good heart.

Why are these five qualities arranged in this order? The first one, a good eye, which means having tolerance for others, is a personal quality. The next two, a good friend and a good neighbor, involve other people, while the last two, seeing ahead and a good heart, are, once again, personal. Why aren't all the personal traits grouped together?

Perhaps the *mishnah*'s order can teach us to blend these qualities. Utilize a good eye to gain good friends and neighbors. Then, with the help of your friends and community, develop the ability to look ahead and to cultivate a good attitude.

When we meet new people, do we take the opportunity to befriend them? There is a purpose to your meeting. Why did Hashem cause the two of you to meet?

Some objectives come to mind:

➢ You can fulfill the mitzvah to love every fellow Jew.

➢ You have an opportunity to "learn from every person" (see *Avos* 4:1).

➢ Perhaps you can be of help to this person, by giving him encouragement, advice, and maybe even some practical assistance.

Learn to always see the good in others. Help them feel better about themselves. Provide them with encouragement. Put others and their needs first.

When you meet someone even for a short period of time, you can apply the teaching, "If not now, when?" (*Avos* 1:14). You can offer a single phrase of encouragement that will echo in

# New Acquaintances

that person's mind forever, transforming his life.

Consider saying: "I sense that you have great potential to achieve in your chosen field," "I like your smile; you make me feel good," "I like your tie. It's my favorite color," or "The Torah insight that you shared with me hit the spot. I will share it with others."

Chapter 20

# "Peace Offering"

*Be first to greet every person.*

(*Avos* 4:20)

The *mishnah*'s word for "greet" is *b'shlom*, from the word *shalom*, meaning peace, harmony, and perfection. To set the right tone for every encounter, we need to avoid statements that may lead to suspicion, fear, or mistrust and instead put the other person at ease with peaceful words.

*For the sake of my brothers and friends, I shall speak of peace....*

(*Tehillim* 122:8)

In every situation, we need to find soothing and appropriate words, but the timing must be right. The halachah teaches that when going to comfort a mourner, one should not begin to speak until the mourner initiates the conversation. This is a form of comfort without the use of words. When the mourning is too intense, we are taught not to even attempt to offer any words of comfort (*Avos* 4:23). Similarly, we are taught, "Do not offer words of appeasement while someone is exploding in anger" (ibid.).

When we speak, we always need to avoid the negative and stick to the positive. We need to avoid *lashon hara*, complaining, and rudeness. In *Tehillim* it says, "Who desires life and loves good days? Guard your tongue from bad and your lips from speaking evil" (*Tehillim* 34:13).

We are not perfect. At times we slip up and say the wrong things. But for our opening words, for that first impression, we should endeavor to always greet others in a pleasant, peaceful manner. One insensitive remark at the beginning can ruin a potentially important long-term friendship.

Chapter 21

# Heads or Tails

We have a mitzvah to love every Jew. The *mishnah*, "Be first to greet every person," will get you into conversation with many types of people. But how much time can you spend with everyone you meet? How many friends are you supposed to have?

The *mishnah* continues:

*Be a tail to lions, and do not be the head of foxes.*

(Avos 4:20)

On the night of Rosh HaShanah we all pray, "May we be a head, not a tail." How do we understand the teaching of this Mishnah?

The answer is that we should associate with those who are greater than we, those who will help us become greater. We are striving to become a "head" of lions, a leader among great people. If we associate only with foxes, less spiritually developed people, we will have no room for growth.

We need to learn from all people (*Avos* 4:1), and every friendship is valuable. But at the same time, we should keep in mind that there are certain people who have much more to teach us than others. Time is precious and we have to utilize every moment the best way possible.

How can we make the most of our encounters with others? Prepare yourself with questions to ask the "lions" you encounter and lessons to share with "foxes." Don't just say anything that comes to mind! Always be prepared with Torah lessons from the parashah, questions on prayer or halachah issues, *daf yomi* insights. There is plenty of source material available if you look for it. Your day-to-day encounters with others can improve immeasurably when you focus on living a life of growth and inspiration.

Chapter 22

# Answering Questions

Often when you meet someone new you are asked, "Where are you from?" You can give a short-form answer, for example, "I'm from Staten Island, New York."

But you can also give a longer answer that will help fuel further conversation. For example, I can say, "I'm from a small town in Staten Island called 'Pleasant Plains.' It is the location of the Yeshiva of Staten Island, which is headed currently by HaRav Reuven Feinstein, *shlita*. Interestingly enough, of all the names of the local towns, this one is most suited for a yeshivah that studies Torah, which is called '*Darchei Noam*,' the ways of pleasantness!"

Of course, your particular response should always be geared to the type of person you're speaking with.

In the book of *Yonah*, the Prophet Yonah is aboard a ship that is threatening to capsize. The others on the ship ask him five questions: "Why are we having trouble? What is your job? Where do you come from? What is your land? Which nation do you come from?" (*Yonah* 1:8).

In response, Yonah says, "I'm a Jew, and I fear Hashem, the God of the Heavens, who created the sea and dry land" (ibid., 9). Although Yonah answered only two of the five questions, he gave his questioners the exact information they were seeking.

At the same time, this response gives us food for thought. What do we stand for? When someone asks us where we come from and what our job is, do we give an automatic response or do we recognize that we should strive to serve Hashem and that our job is one means of accomplishing our goals in this world?

You can say, "I sell shoes," or you can say, "I help people fill their footwear needs." When you describe how you help people, you are developing your job in an admirable, positive way and developing more dedication and joy for your work.

When you are asked about your occupation, consider what interest the questioner might have in you and your work skills. They will be appreciative and inspired, and your conversation will be off to a good start. Prepare a few responses to the question "What do you do?" to use depending on the questioner's needs.

## Chapter 23
# Picking Up Clues

*Do not be disrespectful to any person, and do not push aside any matter....*

(Avos 4:3)

What is the connection between these two messages? On one level we can say that when you are trying to develop a connection with someone else, you should not overlook anything that he says.

Look for clues to help you build up the person's self-esteem. People often mention points that seem inconsequential, but if you train yourself to be alert for clues of what the other person cares about, you can zero in on them and develop a meaningful conversation. An unusual reference, any mention of a place, time, person, or thing, can serve as a topic of conversation.

"One mitzvah leads to another" (ibid., 2). The more respectful you are to another person, the more topics of conversation you will find to discuss.

> *One who is disrespectful to something will be harmed by it.*
>
> (*Mishlei* 13:13)

When we ignore information or become so absorbed in ourselves that we do not really acknowledge the existence and needs of others, we are bound to miss out on many opportunities in life. When Moshe Rabbeinu came across a burning bush that was not being consumed by the fire, he was curious. He investigated the spectacle and was then asked by Hashem to take on leadership of the Jewish people, thus changing the world forever (*Shemos*, ch. 3).

There is a pattern that links together the first four *mishnayos* of the fourth chapter of *Avos*:

1. Who is wise? He who learns from every person.
2. One mitzvah leads to another.

## Picking Up Clues

3. There is no person who does not have his time.

4. Be very, very humble.

When you meet someone, you can learn so much if you ask him sincerely about his life. Turn the spotlight on him. You will grow more by listening than by talking.

When you show an interest in the other person, this mitzvah will naturally lead to appreciating him more and recognizing his significance, for "there is no person who does not have his time." Do not show off your own talents and abilities — rather, focus on his.

It is important to remember that a person stands for much more than his job. Be careful when asking what someone does for a living; he might be embarrassed because he is currently out of work, has just left *kollel* to enter the regular workforce, or is in some similarly awkward position. Some suggest asking instead, "How do you spend your time?"

When someone tells you what he does for a living, tell him what an important job it is. For example, if he sells real estate, you can comment, "You help people find the right homes for their needs." People will always respond positively when they sense that you respect them and their interests.

## Chapter 24

# Word Power

One of the most powerful forces in the arena of acquiring friends is word power. "One who expresses negative words is a fool" (*Mishlei* 10:18).

Besides the obvious prohibition of speaking lashon hara, the Torah forbids us to make jokes at another person's expense. Teasing and other forms of verbal abuse are hurtful, and sinful.

In *Pesachim* (3b), the Gemara teaches that one should always use "clean and kindly words in one's speech." Besides being sensitive to others and avoiding hurting their feelings, we are also taught to avoid reporting bad news. One should not even say, "The wheat crop has failed." Rather, he should say, "Last year's wheat crop was excellent."

When you speak in a refined way, the Gemara informs us, you will merit great benefits. Foolish talk is the sign of a fool, while wise speech will help you develop into a wiser and greater person. This explains why people with better communication skills are more successful in life.

> *The words of the wise, when spoken gently, are accepted.*
>
> (*Koheles* 9:17)

People will respect you more when you speak in a gentle, thoughtful way. They will think of you as kind and intelligent and will desire your friendship. Discuss things in a positive light, using words such as *pure*, *righteous*, *glorious*, and *remarkable*, and you will add flavor and punch to your relationships.

> *One who removes his ears from listening to Torah his prayers will also be considered an abomination.*
>
> (*Mishlei* 28:9)

Hashem deals with us measure for measure. When we reject His Torah, we run the risk that He will reject our prayers. Hashem speaks to us through the Torah; thus, learning Torah is the same as listening to Hashem. When we pray, He listens to us.

Let us learn from this an approach to communication. If someone shares a *d'var Torah* or story which you know already, do not snap, "I heard that already." Why spoil their enjoyment in sharing the idea? Perhaps you will gain some new insight from their telling.

If you react hastily, Hashem can say to you, "Why can't you listen to a review of My holy words? Have you studied the entire Torah 101 times yet? By the way, the prayers you recited today seem very similar to the ones you said yesterday. Should I turn them down, measure-for-measure, because I heard them already?"

Show respect for another person and let him feel important by sharing his *d'var Torah*. Even if he senses that you have heard it, you can say, "I heard it so long ago that I don't remember it clearly" or "I'd like to hear it from your perspective." Think over the idea with more depth and clarity and compliment the person telling it to you for his delivery, enthusiasm, or understanding.

## Chapter 25

# Getting Help

*The world stands on three things: Torah, avodah, and kindness.*

(*Avos* 1:2)

There are four ways we can help others: physically, financially, verbally, and mentally. (See *Hilchos Dei'os* 7:5.) Everyone around us needs help in some of these ways. We must do our best to discern others' needs and offer assistance whenever we can.

But sometimes we ourselves need help. When we ask someone for a favor, there are two ways to voice the request: 1) "I need help," or 2) "Can you please help me?"

The second approach will most likely get a more positive response because you are putting the other person first. By recognizing the other person, you make him feel better about himself.

When you begin sentences with the word *you*, you are giving honor to others. The results will be immediate and obvious. You will find people reacting with more eagerness and pleasantness, and you will be impressed and amazed by the results.

(Take note how many times the word *you* was used in the last paragraph. Did it make you sit up in your chair?)

After we receive help, the next step is to say "thank you."

> *It is good to give thanks to Hashem, and to sing praise to Your Name, Exalted One. To relate Your kindness in the morning and Your faithfulness in the evening.... Because You make me happy with Your activities, I sing about Your handiwork. How great are Your deeds, Hashem, how profound are Your thoughts!*
>
> (*Tehillim* 92:2-6)

The thanks we give to Hashem is a model for how we must thank our fellowman. Do not utter a brief "thank you" and turn away. Explain why you are thanking — sing the message. Express your appreciation of the favor sincerely and earnestly.

"Thank you for being so understanding."

"Thank you for your encouragement."

"Thank you for waiting so patiently."

"Thank you for smiling."

"Thank you for being so caring and loving."

"Thank you for asking."

"Thank you for being such a good friend!"

## Chapter 26

# Praising Properly

When a person feels that you appreciate and respect him, it means more to him than anything else. Praise and compliments are two ways of showing people they are important to you.

As with all mitzvos, we need to know how to do this mitzvah properly, with the right wording, for the right reasons and motivation, and at the right time.

In order to compliment people properly, we need to be well versed in many of the laws of *Sefer Chafetz Chaim*. Avoid statements that may have negative implications, such as, "You're looking great. You must know where all the good kosher restaurants are!" This may be a form of *avak lashon hara* (since it implies that the person eats too much).

## Chapter 27

# On the Phone

We discussed earlier how to greet someone when meeting them in person — smiling, turning our face, and showing interest and concern. But when we communicate over the telephone, these techniques may not be possible. We need to somehow compensate for the missing ingredients.

"Hearing is not as good as seeing" (*Rosh Hashanah* 22b). One can form an impression when he speaks to you over the phone which is not always accurate. The warm smile and the interested expression are difficult to transmit over the wires. You have to say much more to compensate. Spell things out. Dramatize and accentuate your words. Translate your feelings into words and sounds.

Tell your phone friend, "I will not interrupt our discussion by accepting any call-waiting clicks while speaking with you." Comment on what he says: "What a great idea," or "Wow, that is funny!" Use more compliments and words of caring, and say his name more often than you would in person.

However, there are also benefits to speaking over the phone. Without the person's face in front of you, it can be easier for you to think. Contemplate how you can be more concerned for the person's welfare. Let him know that you appreciate his call. Show through your words that you take him seriously. Put a smile in your voice and on your face, and they will sense your good mood.

Smiling is in a sense even greater when the person does not see you because Hashem does. You are fulfilling the precept to "walk modestly with Hashem" (*Michah* 6:8).

To make the person on the other end of the line feel special, you can say something like "How nice to hear from you" or "I've been planning to call you." Show warmth, energy, and enthusiasm to every caller.

Even when you have no time to speak, there is no excuse for not greeting the caller warmly and then saying, "I'm so sorry, I wish I could speak more with you now, but..." or "I'd be happy to schedule a time to speak with you."

Rav Moshe Feinstein, *zt"l*, would always stand up whenever he would speak to Rav Yonasan Steif, *zt"l*, via the phone. When he was asked why, he explained that he was standing out of respect for Reb Yonasan, who was a great *poseik* from the previous generation.

Reb Yonasan may never have known of Reb Moshe's practice, but that doesn't matter. Reb Moshe knew what he was doing and why, and Hashem certainly knew it, too.

Chapter 28

# Timing and Courtesy

One of the most critical issues in dealing with people over the phone is timing. We have mentioned above that there are times when we should avoid comforting or even being near others. With the phone barrier, it is difficult at times to discern a person's state of mind.

Begin a conversation with the question, "Is it convenient for you to speak now?" or "Do you have a minute to discuss something?" You may have great information for the other person, but bad timing can spoil everything. Unless you ask, you don't know if the person was sleeping, eating, learning, about to leave, or snowed under a load of work.

Be sensitive to the other person's needs. If

he says, "I don't have much time, but what do you want?" don't say what you called for! Just ask for a better time. Keep in mind what Queen Esther did with Achashveirosh. She had invited him to a party, but when he asked for her request, she asked for another party. Set an appointment for a convenient time.

Similarly, don't put a long dissertation as a message on your answering machine. You might be wasting the precious time of others who need to leave you a message but don't have the time to listen to your jokes. Leave a short, friendly, and neutral message. Consider: if you cause ten people to waste one minute each, you have wasted ten precious minutes of life.

It is also important to return people's calls promptly. Show consideration for other people's needs.

When you leave a message on other people's machines you are also taking up their time. Is your message intelligent, to the point, brief, and positive?

If you call someone and the conversation is

interrupted by a call-waiting click or another phone ringing, consider saying, "I don't mind waiting while you answer your other call." Although they may respond, "I don't need to take it," you are doing a *chesed* by considering their needs.

Learn to be sensitive to what is going on in your caller's corner. The more careful you are with other people's time, the more they will appreciate you and your call.

Chapter 29

# Six Questions

As we discussed above, Rabbeinu Yonah teaches that we need friends for learning, improved mitzvah performance, and advice. Do our friends fill these needs adequately? Let us ask six practical questions on the topic of acquiring friends.

- Who: Who are my friends? Do I have good learning partners? Do I have competent people from whom to ask advice?
- What: What do I need to do to present myself and my needs to my friends?
- When: When is a good time for me to find the right people?
- Where: Where are the people that I need to meet and get to know?

➤ Why: Why are these efforts necessary?

➤ How: How should I follow up on initial meetings and develop a positive long-term relationship? Should I phone, send handwritten notes, or use e-mail?

When you know what type of friendships you are looking to develop, you will have an idea where and how to discover them. The right shuls and yeshivos are the obvious places for fulfilling these objectives, but we should not overlook other gathering places such as *simchos*.

Chapter 30

# Choosing Friends

Each of us is responsible for our individual growth, and by interacting with others we grow more and accomplish more. When we seek out friends, we must look for people who will help us achieve our goals, not those who might pull us away from them. How do we do this?

When you find yourself in a group of people, at a bar mitzvah, a wedding, or any other *simchah*, you can utilize the opportunity to develop friendships. Look around for the right type of person to approach. Ask yourself: *Who, of these people, would be most beneficial for me to get to know? Who could I learn most from? Who would I enjoy talking to?* Someone talking on a cell phone or engrossed in his meal is not a good choice, since he will not be able to pay attention to you.

Listen to conversations. Someone discussing Torah topics is probably a good candidate. If the discussion involves a topic that you know something about or have unresolved questions on, speak up — volunteer information or ask for help. Avoid people who are talking frivolously or gossiping. By striking up a conversation with someone nearby, you may gain a dear friend, an important business contact, and even just one Torah insight that can enhance your life tremendously.

Sometimes, you can sense that a particular person can change your life. Prepare yourself to approach him, break the ice, and develop a relationship.

When we look at a crowd, we notice specific individuals. Everyone gravitates to different types of people. The ones who stand out to us may have special qualities which will shine out as we seek to discover them.

Before you go to a *simchah*, you can decide

# Choosing Friends

that you will leave it with your life enhanced in some way. You can use the techniques we've discussed throughout this book to either find and acquire a good friend or to practice the skills you need to succeed at it in the near future. Don't wait for others to approach you. Take action and Hashem will help you make it happen.

Keep in mind the *basics*:

- **B** e alert, look around.
- **A** re you from this area? (Good first question.)
- **S** mile and be friendly.
- **I** s there time to talk a little about…?
- **C** an we stay in contact?
- **S** mile again, to thank Hashem for sending you a friend.

Chapter 31

# Forgiveness

*Anyone who passes over his personal feelings to forgive others is forgiven for all his sins.*
(Rosh HaShanah 17a)

This statement is defined by Rashi as referring to people who don't keep track of petty mistakes and offenses. Rather, they forgive and forget.

When we deal with people, we are subject to misunderstandings, accidental insults, and minor mishaps. The best way to deal with them is to say, "It's nothing" and ignore the distraction completely. It may be difficult, but it is worth it.

*Never build up your own honor at the expense of others.*

(Rambam, *Hilchos Dei'os* 6:3)

When we pass over our ego, when we forego

# Forgiveness

our pride and forgive others, we will be successful in both making and keeping friends. The greatest motivation is the Gemara's assurance, "Anyone who passes over his personal feelings to forgive others is forgiven for all his sins."

When we don't keep tabs with others, Hashem will forgive us, measure for measure. Imagine a great scorecard in Heaven. We can boost our score by developing friendships and keeping them. As we perfect ourselves, Hashem makes it worth our while, in this world and in the World to Come!

You do not get to the top by yourself; Hashem has designed this world so that as you help others achieve you gain more and more. We need to practice thinking more about others and their needs. When we focus on th big picture and not get caught up in small details, we will gain more friends the Torah way.

# Part 2

# Ten Steps to Shidduchim

# A Lifetime Friendship

# Introduction

There is a phenomenon occurring in today's *frum* community: the growing number of older singles. We are not going to attempt to analyze the situation and give possible reasons for it. Rather, we are going to offer some practical steps to self-improvement and relationship building, which will, *b'ezras Hashem*, lead to finding the right *shidduch* and getting married. (These steps are also beneficial for maintaining one's marriage in a positive, loving way.)

It is not good for a person to be unmarried (see *Bereishis* 2:18). Rav Avigdor Miller, *zt"l*, often stressed that a person cannot achieve his or her primary goal in life, spiritual perfection, without the assistance of his or her *eizer kenegdo* (helpmate).

Don't we all know this? Certainly, but review is always helpful. The Gemara teaches that even better than learning a subject 100 times is learning it 101 times (*Chagigah* 9b).

Let us hope and pray to Hashem that the information in this work will be helpful to singles, their parents, their friends, and all of *klal Yisrael* so that we may be privileged to attend many weddings in the near future.

Step 1

# Begin with Thanks

*Come, let us sing to Hashem, let us shout with joy to the Source of our salvation. Let us greet Him with thanksgiving...for Hashem is great.*
(Tehillim 95:1–3)

You need not wait until that great day of celebration to praise Hashem. Jump-start the process by starting at the end: Hashem has already prepared a wonderful *shiduch* for you. Thank Him for it now. You have been praying for it, and you are becoming more and more ready, so thank Him now for His assistance.

When people work for a certain goal for a long time and are unsuccessful, they sometimes get depressed and see only negative. We tend to forget the overwhelming majority of our life, which has been successful. Be grateful to

Hashem for the eyes with which you see, the ears with which you hear, hands with which you write, and a voice with which you speak.

Be grateful to Hashem for your parents, siblings, friends, and relatives. Learn to say, "Thank You, Hashem, for my family setting. Please provide every member of my family with what he/she needs." The more we thank Hashem for the kindnesses that He provides us with, the more He will provide for us.

Are we looking at the world with a bitter perspective, noting only what we are lacking, or are we grateful to Hashem for the abundance we are presently enjoying? Begin today to be more grateful for everything you have. Perhaps start a program of identifying one specific thing each day to be thankful for. Your new attitude can become the turning point in your life! A person who is constantly thankful develops a personality that attracts others.

> *How can I repay Hashem for all of His kindness to me? I will raise a cup as thanks for His salvation.*
>
> (*Tehillim* 116:12–13)

# Begin with Thanks

When we focus on repaying Hashem for all of His kindness, we will merit Hashem's help so that we can continue to proclaim our thanks for His salvation.

Every time you hear of a new engagement, you can be happy if you realize that Hashem is demonstrating what He will do for you soon. You can say, "Thank You, Hashem, for my *shidduch*!" This will increase your trust in Hashem and help you pray with greater patience and with faith that your prayer will soon become a reality.

## Step 2

# Seeing the Future

*Who is wise? He who foresees the future.*
(*Tamid* 32a)

We cannot predict the future. However, we can see clearly that certain types of behavior will not be beneficial and are even harmful to our development.

We learned in the previous chapter that a person should continually be thankful for what he has and for what he will have soon. If you focus on what you lack and on how lonely you are, you set in motion a self-fulfilling prophecy: you will be more lonely. However, if you "see" the future and focus on good things happening, you will embark on a positive self-fulfilling prophecy, and good things will happen to you sooner. Hashem helps those who strive to improve.

# Seeing the Future

The Gemara teaches that a person is obligated to thank Hashem with one hundred blessings daily (*Menachos* 43b). When you count your blessings, they increase and multiply.

> *Pleasant words are like a honeycomb, sweet to the soul and [promoting] health to the bones.*
> (*Mishlei* 16:24)

> *Life and death are in the power of the tongue.*
> (Ibid. 18:21)

We should not waste words. Idle or cynical words, so-called jokes, are not in line with positive thoughts. Focus on a positive future. If you keep saying to yourself, "There's no chance. I'm never going to get married," you may slide into a rut and never get out of it. If, however, you say to yourself, "Hashem loves me and has a great *shidduch* for me, which was prepared for me before I was born" (see *Sotah* 2a), it will happen sooner.

A note of caution: While it is very beneficial to foresee the future and focus on the good that will happen, one must not ignore the present. Some singles schedule numerous dates in close proximity in order to meet as many people as possible. This may cause them not to seriously consider each person they meet as a potential spouse, believing that someone better is just around the corner — someone taller, wiser, more learned, better looking, or thinner. If a person dates this way, he fails to focus on the unique person right before him.

"The eyes of a fool are focused to the end of the world" (*Mishlei* 17:24). It is not necessary to look to the ends of the earth for your *shidduch*. Stop and think! Carefully evaluate what you already have.

Closely related to this topic is the importance of judging every person positively. (See *Avos* 1:6, and our book *How to Judge People*.) You will not summarily discard the person in front of you in your haste to meet the next person on the *shadchan*'s list if you give your current date the benefit of the doubt. Do not judge the actions of your new date instantly. It works both ways: if you give your date the benefit of the doubt, your date will do the same for you.

Step 3

# Growing Younger

When people grow older, they tend to start thinking that they have nothing more to learn. They have a stable routine and they have seen everything. This type of attitude translates into a lack of enthusiasm for life.

There is so much in the world to learn, so much to do and accomplish. Loss of enthusiasm for living is an affliction we must avoid at all cost. A wise person learns from everyone, all the time (*Avos* 4:1). The longer we live, the more we should develop an eagerness and excitement for life.

A person who lacks enthusiasm cannot be a good listener. One who is anxious to learn and hear what the other person has to say will be able to develop a better relationship. If you talk too much about yourself, you will not learn more about your date or foster enthusiasm for him or her. Listening and learning will be far more beneficial.

When we are willing to learn from others, we will be able to commit to caring about another person in a way that will forge two individuals into a single unit. When two people strive to help and trust each other, there is potential for growth. It is not necessary for two people pursuing a *shidduch* to have identical goals. In a successful relationship, when you want something for yourself, your mate wants it for you, too.

But what if you never get that far in your *shidduch* dating? After one or two dates, the story is over. How can you get to the next stage?

Give the other person a chance. The person who set you up thinks there is some potential in the relationship. Listen to what your date has to say. Do not judge him by his external appearance. Try to determine why the person in front of you is worth knowing, and you will, with Hashem's help, be successful.

Step 4

# Be Positive

If you are positive and upbeat, people will respond in kind. We have learned about how important it is to greet all people with joy. If you speak with more kindness in your voice, your attitude toward others will improve. You will also help the people you interact with relax by using gentler phrases.

Just as it is important to be positive, it is important to cause other people to have a positive opinion of you. What can you do to create a positive image? Begin by keeping your word. When you arrange a date, be on time. If you experience an unavoidable delay, be considerate and contact the other person to explain the situation.

Show integrity and character in all of your

dealings. If you go to a restaurant, treat the waiter or waitress in a way that reflects well on you. When people see that they can trust you, they will look forward to seeing you again.

If you have been dating for a number of years and have been unsuccessful thus far, it's time to reevaluate the situation. In order to find the right *shidduch*, you may have to do things you have never done before. You need clear, challenging, and realistic goals and plans to accomplish them. You need to work on developing yourself daily, step by step.

> *On the road a person wants to travel, in it, he will be led.*
>
> (*Makos* 10b)

There are very few limitations to what you can do or become when you recognize this principle. You have reserves of potential talent waiting to be uncovered and released. When you uncover them, you will be a more complete and more satisfied person.

There are functions that you were put on this earth to accomplish. Only you can achieve these functions. When, *b'ezras Hashem*, you find your *shidduch*, you and your mate can together unlock your combined potential in all the various parts of your lives. Satisfaction, fulfillment, and happiness will result.

We don't know what our ultimate mission in life is and how it will develop. Our Sages teach that Boaz, a great tzaddik who had sixty children throughout his long life, did not fulfill his ultimate purpose until his last day. When he married Rus and Oveid was conceived, Boaz achieved his purpose in life, and he died the next day. Oveid became the seed of royalty, the grandfather of David HaMelech and the ancestor of Mashiach.

Although we don't know when we will be called upon to fulfill our ultimate mission in life, we should prepare for it every day. We can accomplish great things if we try consistently to fulfill our potential.

Step 5

# Self-Discipline

*Who is strong? He who conquers his evil inclination.*

(Avos 4:1)

When we are in control of ourselves, we have a much better chance of finding the right *shidduch*. Be attuned to others and their needs. One of the goals in marriage is to give to one's mate. By practicing this now, you will perfect the qualities you need for a successful marriage.

A suggested way to train yourself for a good marriage is to rehearse for this relationship by going out of your way to make another person happy in your daily life. Choose one friend, relative, or acquaintance and focus on being a good friend to him or her.

If you keep this up every day, you will find yourself moving forward in your desired direction. Slowly but surely your personality will change. You will become less self-centered, more clear-headed, and more friendly, and you will become a finer, better, and gentler person. You will be approached with amazing choices of suitable prospects, in accordance with the principle of *middah keneged middah*: how you act toward others is how Hashem will cause others to act toward you.

It will take discipline, but it will be well worth your while. "According to the difficulties, the rewards will increase" (*Avos* 5:26).

As you strengthen your fulfillment of the mitzvah to "love your friend as yourself" (*Vayikra* 19:18), you will achieve a level of strength in relating to others that will prepare you for a great *shidduch*.

Step 6

# Rejoice

After discussing the benefits of learning from others (Step 1) and the benefits of self-control (Step 5), we can examine another lesson contained in the same *mishnah*: "Who is wealthy? He who rejoices with his portion" (*Avos* 4:1).

People who have, thus far, been unsuccessful in finding the right *shidduch* may think that their married friends have received a better break in life: they must have better looks, better jobs, nicer families, nicer personalities, and more money.

Such thinking will only hold you back. You need to look into yourself to discover who you really are. What have you done in the past that was enjoyable? What has been your greatest success in life up till now? What work do you love? What are your interests? What are your dreams for accomplishing in life?

If you do not like the answers you gave to the above questions, now is a good time to reflect on your situation and make a sound commitment to change. Hashem tells us, "Open your mouth wide and I will fill it up" (*Tehillim* 81:11). What is right for you? What will make you truly happy? If you are having difficulty getting started, pray to Hashem for help. We should begin every project with prayer and continue asking for help with every step.

When you think about who you are, you should "rejoice with your portion." Thank Hashem sincerely for all that He has done for you. You got up this morning. You live in a warm and comfortable environment. You can breathe, eat, walk, see, talk, and smell.

Once you do this, you will be more ready to ask Hashem for something more: the *shidduch* that is just right for you. Open your mouth wide (figuratively) to ask Hashem for help in meeting that someone special who will match your needs perfectly.

Step 7

# Relating to Others

Let us now explore the next step to achieving the right *shidduch*: "Who is honored? He who honors others" (*Avos* 4:1).

Train yourself to bestow more honor and respect on others. How can this be done?

1. Look for and find the good in every person and every situation.

2. Avoid arguments and strive to always get along with others. You do not have to agree with everything others say. There may be differences of opinion. However, you must always demonstrate that you like people and respect them and that you value their opinions.

3. Forgive those who slight you. Do not bear grudges. Life is too precious to waste on petty thoughts.

If you want people to be impressed with you, the trick is not to tell them outright how great you are. The Mishnah teaches: "Who is honored? He who honors others." When you are interested in other people, they will be interested in you. When you respect others and admire them, they respond in kind. "As water reflects one's face, so a person's heart reflects another's" (*Mishlei* 27:19).

The Hebrew word for honor, *kavod*, is related to the word *kaveid*, heavy. One aspect to honoring others is appreciating that each person has a heavy bundle of qualities that deserve recognition and admiration. Another aspect is to realize that almost every person you meet has a heavy load of issues he is dealing with. Everyone needs encouragement, compliments, and recognition.

The mitzvah of honoring others can be divided into two parts:

1. Stop tearing people down. Don't say or do anything that may lower someone's self-esteem. Negative attitudes are hard to

conceal and tend to be carried over to other settings, like dates. One who engages in this type of activity is destined to receive similar treatment, *middah keneged middah*.

2. Say only those things that build people up and make them feel important. Boost their self-esteem, and you will receive the same treatment.

# Step 8

# Be Organized

*Orderliness denotes virtue.*
(Rav Avigdor Miller, *Journey into Greatness*, p. 329)

Orderliness is needed in all areas of life, but especially in *shidduchim*. Know what you are looking for in a *shidduch* and present yourself in an orderly fashion. When you know where you are headed, you can get there on target.

The Talmud teaches that messiness and uncleanliness are causes of poverty (*Shabbos* 62b). This is reflected in the name of the angel in charge of wealth: "cleanliness" (*Pesachim* 111b).

Our environment reflects on what we stand for and what we are striving to accomplish. A clean home shows that one cares about himself and his health. An organized desktop is a sign that one is focused on his work and on his plans to achieve.

If you take the time to be organized, you will be able to accomplish more with clarity, focus, and concentration. Plan what you want to say before each date. Present your topic in a clear, vivid, and interesting way so that your date will ask more. Don't waste his or her time with muddled, unclear thoughts.

You are here in this world for a specific purpose. Hashem has granted you with a soul and the ability to choose friends to walk through life with. If you think through who you are and what you want out of life and present yourself in a clear way, you will succeed in finding your predestined mate.

Each person has unlimited potential. Your orderliness within will help in your interactions with others. You can develop yourself so that you are on a higher level, and then you will be able to form the relationship that will last a lifetime, to continuously grow even greater.

Step 9

# Five Keys to Improvement

We have discussed many different techniques that will improve our interpersonal relationships. It is crucial to keep these techniques in mind when you meet a *shadchan* or a potential marriage partner. Five keys to improving your dating are set out below.

## Smile More

When you smile at others, they feel valuable, more worthwhile. Scientists say that it only takes 13 muscles to smile, but it takes 112 muscles to frown. Why waste all that effort? Relax and smile more.

We all look nicer when we smile. If you want to make a good impression when you meet someone, smile at him or her! In addition, a *shadchan* who remembers you with a smile on your face will be more inclined to help you and will return your calls more quickly.

*Pirkei Avos* teaches the importance of greeting others with a smile in three different places (*Avos* 1:15, 3:16, and 4:20). Even when you find it difficult to smile, when you are not in the mood, you must force yourself to smile. Everyone will benefit — including you!

## Avoid Arguments

If you win all of your arguments, you will lose all of your friends. The Gemara teaches, "A person should agree easily with others on general matters [that do not interfere with Torah principles]" (*Kesubos* 17a). When a *shadchan* makes a suggestion that you don't like, you can turn it down without an argument. The same principle can be applied to a *shidduch*. When a date says something you disagree with, you can change the topic without arguing.

It is important to get along with other people. "He who is pleasing to his fellowmen is pleasing also to Hashem" (*Avos* 3:13). Avoiding arguments is a form of promoting peace, which will cause people to appreciate you more. "Be of the disciples of Aharon, loving peace and pursuing peace" (*Avos* 1:12).

## Say "Please" and "Thank You"

The little things that people do are what others tend to notice and remember. When you thank *shadchanim* for their time and efforts on your behalf, they will gladly keep you in mind and do more for you. A thank-you note for their favors will keep your name at the top of their minds.

A *shadchan* usually deserves a note and maybe even a gift for setting you up, even if the *shidduch* did not develop further. The *shadchan* may have invested much time, effort, money (in long-distance calls), thoughts, and feelings on your behalf. (Incidentally, don't wait too long in getting back to the *shadchan* about how your date went. Show that you do care!)

Even if this *shidduch* was not for you, your thoughtfulness may result in someone remembering you and suggesting you to a friend or another *shadchan*. The more thankful you are, the more you will receive from Hashem to be thankful for.

## Look for Areas to Compliment Others

Complimenting others will make them feel good about themselves and positive toward you. This applies to both prospective mates and *shadchanim*. If your date is punctual, generous, or courteous, take note of it and mention it to him (and to the *shadchan*). You will be beginning the relationship on a positive note.

When dealing with a *shadchan*, you can compliment him or her, too. Notice his thoughtfulness and persistence, and you will make him feel appreciated.

## Listen Well

Although we've discussed listening many times, it is one of the most important things to keep in mind when you embark on a date. You will never move forward in a relationship unless you focus on listening to the other person.

The words *shema Yisrael*, which we recite at least twice a day, can remind us of the great mitzvah to pay attention to others. How much attention you pay to others is the chief indicator of how important they are to you. When you listen to others, you demonstrate that you care about them, and they in turn will like you more and pay more attention to you.

Step 10

# The Bottom Line

When we simplify matters, it can help wake us up to obvious truths. The first thing to recognize is that everything is in Hashem's hands, and we cannot hope to find a *shidduch* without praying to Him. However, we must also do our *hishtadlus* (efforts). The secret to success in *shidduchim* can be summed up in two forms of *hishtadlus*:

1. Focus on the needs of others. Stop being self-centered and start thinking about other people's needs and concerns. Think of ways to help others. See if you can help someone else find a *shidduch*. Chances are your efforts for others will boomerang back to you, sooner or later.

   The Gemara states: "When one prays

for others for something he himself needs, Hashem will assist him first" (*Bava Kama* 91a). Perhaps you have already been praying for *shidduchim* for friends for years, yet you are still unmarried. Do not give up! "A tzaddik falls seven times, but he keeps on getting up" (*Mishlei* 24:16).

2. Strive for improvement. Get busy working on yourself and your goals for improvement. Develop the unique talents Hashem implanted within you. You can become more positive and more effective, and you will find a better *shidduch*.

May Hashem help you find a great *shidduch* and succeed in helping others to find *shidduchim* also.

# Small Books.

TARGUM PRESS Books